# THE SECOND WORLD
## IN PHOTOGRAPHS

# 1944

# THE SECOND WORLD WAR AT SEA IN PHOTOGRAPHS

# 1944

PHIL CARRADICE

AMBERLEY

First published 2016

Amberley Publishing
The Hill, Stroud
Gloucestershire, GL5 4EP

www.amberley-books.com

Copyright © Phil Carradice 2016

The right of Phil Carradice to be identified as the Author
of this work has been asserted in accordance with the
Copyrights, Designs and Patents Act 1988.

All rights reserved. No part of this book may be reprinted
or reproduced or utilised in any form or by any electronic,
mechanical or other means, now known or hereafter invented,
including photocopying and recording, or in any information
storage or retrieval system, without the permission in writing
from the Publishers.

British Library Cataloguing in Publication Data.
A catalogue record for this book is available from the British Library.

ISBN 978 1 4456 2253 8 (print)
ISBN 978 1 4456 2276 7 (ebook)

Typeset in 10pt on 12pt Sabon.
Typesetting and Origination by Amberley Publishing.
Printed in the UK.

# Contents

| | |
|---|---|
| Introduction | 7 |
| January | 11 |
| February | 23 |
| March | 34 |
| April | 39 |
| May | 47 |
| June | 54 |
| July | 72 |
| August | 78 |
| September | 83 |
| October | 94 |
| November | 106 |
| December | 115 |

# Introduction

If, as far as the men and women of Britain's armed forces were concerned, the previous five years of war had been a dogged and determined fight for survival, then 1944 was the year when the Allies really began to hit back.

Italy had surrendered and Germany had been pushed out of Africa, but Japanese and German forces were still fighting fiercely, both in the Far East and on the long leg of the Italian peninsula. It was the same at sea, where Russian and Atlantic convoys continued to run and U-boats, albeit in significantly fewer numbers, continued to send merchant ships to the bottom.

In addition to the lurking U-boats and the threat from ships like the *Tirpitz*, the snow, ice and bitter weather continued to be the main enemy for the men of the merchant fleets, as they ploughed through the freezing Arctic waters. To be thrown into that water meant almost instant death, and it was not a prospect that anyone relished.

Stalin's forces were beginning to make significant progress against the German invaders but many of the tanks, supplies and weapons brought to Murmansk and other Russian ports were left untouched on the quayside. Consequently, sailors repeatedly questioned the value and the purpose of the Russian convoys. Despite their doubts, the convoys continued.

Above all, however, the year was marked by an increasing number of amphibious landings on enemy-held territory.

They began in January, with Allied landings at Anzio in southern Italy. Operation Shingle, as the landings were called, was an attempt to bypass or outflank stubborn German resistance. It was hampered by a lack of landing craft, which were deliberately held back ready for the forthcoming D-Day landings, and by a lack of urgency in the higher command. Nevertheless, important lessons were learned – lessons that would be vital in the forthcoming assault on France.

In the Pacific theatre, American forces, with their hold on Guadalcanal now firmly established, began a series of landings on remote, Japanese-held locations such as the Admiralty Islands, Los Negros, Saipan, Guam and Tinian. The landings were carried out by men of the US Marine Corps and were all proceeded by massive naval bombardments.

The effectiveness of such bombardments was limited, with commanders seeming to have forgotten the lessons of the First World War. In most cases, the marines had to wade ashore into a hail of gunfire. Casualties were enormous.

At the end of April, an American training exercise off Slapton Sands in Devon went disastrously wrong. Poor communication led to American landing craft being subjected to friendly fire and when, the following day, a convoy of such vessels was attacked by E-boats, it brought the death total to 946. The truth behind the disaster was kept secret for some time, families of the dead men being told that they had simply died in action.

The Normandy invasion – or the D-Day landings, as they were known – took place just after dawn on 6 June. The weather was unhelpful but, after one twenty-four-hour postponement, General Eisenhower decided to go ahead with the landings on 6 June. The alternative was to delay the operation for another month, and the logistics involved in such a delay did not bear too much thought.

Operation Overlord was the largest seaborne invasion ever organised, with over 2,000 vessels of various types and size involved in getting the troops ashore, ranging from battleships to tiny landing craft. The German defenders were taken by surprise, as most German intelligence predicted that the landings would take place in the Calais area.

The naval bombardment that preceded the landings was, in the main, effective, with battleships, cruisers and destroyers pounding German positions. It was accompanied by repeated heavy aerial assaults. The five landing beaches – code named Gold, Juno, Sword, Utah and Omaha – were along a 50-mile stretch of the Normandy coast, which saw British, American and Canadian soldiers flooding ashore.

The American attacks on Omaha Beach were costly and were held up for a time by stubborn German defence. Over 1,000 GIs died on Omaha before the Americans were able to establish their beachhead but, by the end of the day, nearly 150,000 Allied troops were ashore and Hitler's much-vaunted Atlantic Wall had been breached.

Over the days following 6 June, thousands more troops, as well as supplies and heavy armour, were landed on the Normandy beaches. Until the Allies were able to capture one of the French ports, much of this came over the Mulberry harbours, artificial jetties and caissons. These had been constructed in Britain and towed across the Channel in a unique and highly effective feat of engineering.

Meanwhile, in the Pacific, US Marines continued their landings, inching ever closer to the Japanese mainland. A meeting between President Roosevelt and General MacArthur on 26 July saw heated debate. The General's much-publicised wish to return to the Philippines – he had left, earlier in the war, declaring, 'I shall return' – was passed over in favour of bypassing certain islands and, thereby, isolating them from the Japanese supply chain.

At the end of August, as Allied land forces pushed relentlessly eastwards across Europe, the Kriegsmarine was forced to order the scuttling of those U-boats that had been left isolated in French ports. On 22 August, Admiral Donitz, realising that the naval war in the Black Sea was virtually over, also ordered the scuttling of German ships in that theatre of war.

It was not all one-way traffic, however. On 15 September, a German frogman attack on the floodgates of Antwerp caused significant damage and made the port unusable for large vessels for six weeks or more. A month later, the Australian cruiser *Canberra*, along with the USS *Franklin*, was seriously damaged by Japanese bombers during Allied attacks on Formosa.

On 15 October, the battleship *Tirpitz* was unexpectedly moved from its base in Altafjord to a shallower anchorage in Tromso Fjord, a move that put her 100 miles closer to RAF bases in Britain. It was a signal for further attacks on the battleship, which, by her mere presence in Norwegian waters, represented a significant threat to the Russian convoys.

On 12 November, an attack by Lancaster bombers saw three Tallboy bombs score direct hits on the *Tirpitz*. The giant vessel turned over and capsized within twelve minutes of being hit. Very few of the crew managed to scramble to safety, with over 1,000 being drowned or killed by the bombs. The sinking of the *Tirpitz* effectively ended the activities of Germany's surface fleet – what little resistance that remained in the Kriegsmarine now rested largely in the hands of the U-boats.

Out in the Pacific, with the spectre of defeat looming ever larger, the Japanese resorted to making suicide attacks on American and British ships. These kamikaze attacks were both effective and terrifying for Allied sailors who, with the war now moving to a conclusion, had a redoubled interest in getting home safely. The Japanese pilots, obviously, took a different view.

On 25 November, kamikaze attacks seriously damaged four aircraft carriers off Luzon. Four days later, there was more success for the Japanese suicide pilots when American ships were attacked during the particularly bloody battle for Leyte. On 13 December, the cruiser *Nashville*, flagship of a force heading for Mindanao, was yet another casualty. The cruiser was seriously damaged and several senior officers were among the casualties.

Despite the kamikaze attacks, the American offensive in the Pacific continued to grind on. It was a brutal and violent campaign but, as 1944 came to an end, it was clear that further fighting would be required before either the Japanese or the German forces were defeated.

# January

On 4 January 1944, the destroyer USS *Jouett* and the cruiser *Omaha* intercepted and sank the German blockade runner *Rio Grande*, which was making its way to the Far East. The *Rio Grande* was almost the last of the German merchant ships trying to bring supplies back to a hard-pressed country. Pictured is the USS *Omaha*.

An American tank rolls down the ramp of its Landing Craft, Tank, onto the beach.

*Opposite above*: Destroyers at sunset, outlined against the disappearing sun.

*Opposite below*: US Marines go over the top during the landings on Tarawa island.

German merchant vessels under attack from British Beaufighters of Coastal Command, 15 January 1944.

Minesweeping trawlers and drifters – an unglamorous but very necessary facet of the war at sea. Mines were sown indiscriminately by all sides during the war. They accounted for numerous ship losses and many deaths; when the war finally did come to an end, sweeping them up would prove to be an onerous task.

A British motor torpedo boat at speed. MTBs were used to attack German shipping around the coast of mainland Europe, and also to counter the threat of the German E-boats.

The escort carrier *Argus*, one of many hastily constructed aircraft carriers made for use on the convoy routes across the Atlantic and into Arctic waters. Basic in design and with limited facilities for crew, they nevertheless carried out useful work in providing air cover for the convoys.

US troops landing at Anzio, 22 January. Largely unopposed, over 50,000 Allied troops were ashore by the following day.

A night bombardment of the Italian coast by the Royal Navy, in support of the Anzio landings.

US warships bombard Japanese positions before another landing in the Pacific.

Italian submarines, serving with the Royal Navy after the Italian surrender.

French anti-aircraft gunners on board a Free French destroyer.

The battleship *King George V* is seen here, framed by the barrels of a pom-pom gun on a British aircraft carrier.

Admiral Raymond Spruance, the American commander of the task force that landed on Kwajalein Atoll in the Pacific on 31 January. It was the first American landing of the year in the Pacific, but others were to follow in quick succession.

US landings on Kwajalein Atoll at the end of January. This shows US Marines wading ashore from their landing craft.

# February

By the beginning of 1944, the significance of air power had made itself clear for the politicians, admirals and generals of all sides; the aircraft carrier had become the most important vessel in naval warfare. Much as they might argue the point, the day of the battleship was almost over. However, landing on the deck of an aircraft carrier, often pitching and rolling in heavy sea, was never easy. Accidents could and did happen. This shows an Albacore torpedo bomber crashed on the flight deck of an aircraft carrier.

A crashed Sea Hornet – in effect, a seaborne Mosquito fighter-bomber – on the deck of its carrier. The nose of the aircraft has been totally smashed and the pilot later died of his injuries.

A and B turrets of a British destroyer, shown here close-up.

The Russian convoys continued throughout 1944. This shows escorts waiting for another convoy to form off the Icelandic coast.

Ice, a perpetual problem for ships on the Russian convoys.

A newly commissioned frigate, one of many new vessels designed and built to help – and eventually replace – the old Flower-class corvettes, which had done such useful work protecting convoys throughout the war.

*Opposite*: The deck of a Thames sailing barge. Coastal traffic continued throughout the war years, with sailing barges, fishing boats and small tramp steamers regularly braving the hazards of U-boats, aerial attack and E-boats to deliver their valuable cargoes.

The British aircraft carrier HMS *Atheling*.

Avenger torpedo bombers taking off from the flight deck of HMS *Trumpeter*.

Due largely to improved aerial escort – from long-distance bombers and escort carriers attached to the convoys – the toll on U-boats became markedly heavier in the opening months of 1944. This aerial view shows one enemy submarine, bombed by a patrolling Sunderland, taking its final dive.

U-boat prisoners, lucky to be alive after their submarine was sunk, come up the gangplank into what was, surely, a welcome captivity.

*Opposite*: The work of rescue tugs went largely unheralded, but the men of these tiny vessels performed heroically, rescuing sailors and towing badly damaged ships into port.

Canadian gunners on HMCS *Prince Robert*.

HMS *Howe*, a KG5-class battleship that was soon to take on the role of British flagship in the Pacific.

# March

War or no war, sailors still found time for entertainment. This shows a boxing match on the deck of one ship.

A crashed Swordfish – the undercarriage has buckled and collapsed.

Refuelling at sea, a delicate and often dangerous operation due to the enemy submarines and aircraft lurking around.

A tanker of the Royal Fleet Auxiliary service prepares to pass a fuel line to a waiting warship. RFA ships were a lifeline for the Royal Navy.

US troops landing in Dutch New Guinea.

HMS *Searcher* with US Wildcat fighters on board.

Gunners firing their shells on HMS *Grenville*.

# April

On 3 April, aircraft from HMS *Victorious* (shown here) and HMS *Furious* bombed the battleship *Tirpitz* in her Norwegian fjord. They scored fourteen hits on the German warship and, eager to protect one of his few remaining surface ships of note, Admiral Donitz promptly forbade her future use against convoys.

The *Tirpitz*, under attack from Allied bombers in April 1944.

The cruiser HMS *Norfolk*, a ship that spent most of the war in northern waters.

Snow was a major problem for any aircraft carrier engaged in the Russian convoys. It would have been hazardous in the extreme for aircraft to even attempt landing or take off when there was this much snow on the deck.

No alternative – crewmen shovel snow from the deck of a British aircraft carrier on convoy duties in the Arctic.

The carrier *Victorious*, shown here in Icelandic waters.

A Swordfish aircraft leaves the deck of its aircraft carrier.

US troops ashore during Operation Tiger off the Devon coast on 27 April. Poor communication led to many deaths from friendly fire, something that was hushed up until after the war. To make matters worse, on 28 April, German E-boats managed to slip past the British escorts and wreak havoc with the landing craft taking part in Operation Tiger. In total, counting the friendly-fire fatalities of the previous day and those sustained in the E-boat attack, 946 American soldiers lost their lives in the disaster.

General Bernard Montgomery, easily Britain's most successful army commander, visits the Home Fleet. He is shown here inspecting the 'Mae West' lifejacket of a Fleet Air Arm pilot.

New weapons, new tactics, forged in the crucible of war – a two-man human torpedo is lowered into the sea.

# May

Swordfish aircraft on the flight deck. Despite its slow speed and decidedly 'stringbag' appearance, the Swordfish torpedo bomber played an important role in air/sea operations throughout the Second World War.

With the Italians beaten, the Mediterranean remained a British preserve. This shows the Mediterranean Fleet in Malta's Grand Harbour.

The triple 21-inch torpedo tubes of a British cruiser.

'Crossing the line' – in other words, passing over the equator – had always been time for fun and celebration when Neptune (usually the oldest petty officer on board) visited; sailors crossing for the first time were dunked and daubed with all manner of foul-smelling concoctions. Wartime or no wartime, the ceremony continued. This shows the certificate awarded to one of the sailors on the *Victorious*, a certain 'Dai Bach', as he was known.

HMS *Chaser*, one of many similar escort carriers on convoy duty. A Swordfish aircraft has just taken off and the observer in the rear cockpit has snapped the picture.

A Beaufighter attack on a German convoy off the coast of Norway – disrupting German supplies of food and equipment was vitally important at this stage of the war.

German U-boats continued to sink Allied ships. This shows survivors from a sunken merchantman swimming in the water, waiting to be rescued.

Merchant Navy sailors or enemy survivors, it was the duty of all Allied ships to pick up survivors. This shows HMS *Wren*, stopped to pick up the crew of a sunken U-boat.

# June

The battleship *King George V*, which in 1944 was still one of the most powerful vessels in the Royal Navy.

The invasion of Europe, Stalin's long-awaited Second Front, began on 6 June 1944. Well over 2,000 ships of varying sizes, from giant battleships to minute landing craft, were involved in getting the invading army ashore on the Normandy beaches. Operation Overlord, to give it the correct name, was the largest seaborne invasion ever attempted.

The USS *Nevada* bombards the shore on 6 June, during the landings on Utah Beach.

US soldiers heading towards Omaha Beach. The landings on Omaha were held up for several hours by dogged German defence but, as evening closed in, the GIs were finally able to gain a tenuous foothold on enemy soil.

*Opposite above*: Approaching Omaha Beach on 6 June.

*Opposite below*: The second American landing beach was Utah and here things went more or less as planned, thousands of soldiers quickly getting ashore.

King George, in naval uniform, visits the ships of the Home Fleet.

The American landings on Saipan began on the morning of 15 June. This shows landing craft heading for the shore.

It seemed to those who watched the D-Day armada as if the sea was totally covered with Allied ships, all of them en route to the Normandy beaches. This aerial view shows just a small part of the invasion fleet.

US troops wade ashore on D-Day.

An artist's impression of the D-Day landings, from a British perspective. This shows British troops landing on Sword Beach.

The naval bombardment that went before the landings was short but brutal in its intensity. This shows a British cruiser firing on enemy positions, just minutes before the landing craft went in.

LCIs (Landing Craft, Infantry) heading towards land.

The troops might do the fighting, but the senior officers were there to watch proceedings. Admiral Ramsey, General Eisenhower and General Montgomery can do little more than stand and wait on board the *Apollo*.

Admiral Cunningham and Air Vice-Marshal Charles Portal, on the bridge of a warship, watching proceedings.

British soldiers going ashore in an American Duck – another new invention that revolutionised amphibious landings.

Gliders, each of them carrying dozens of American and British soldiers of the airborne brigades, pass over the *Warspite* and *Ramillies*. The glider landings were not totally successful, and many of the men in these flimsy aircraft would die during the landing process.

A Bofors gun crew watch as supplies are landed onto the D-Day beaches.

It proved impossible to keep him out of the action – if Churchill had had his way, he would have gone ashore with the first wave on 6 June. This shows the British prime minister with General Montgomery on the invasion beaches, a few days after the landings.

A force of 325 Lancaster bombers raided the port of Le Havre on 14 June. As well as damaging the town and docks, some thirty small vessels were sunk in the harbour.

The American landings on Saipan in the Pacific took place a few weeks after the Normandy invasion, on 15 June. The landings were fiercely contested, as this view of Japanese aircraft and exploding anti-aircraft shells clearly shows.

US Marines land on Saipan.

The Battle of the Philippine Sea began on 19 June, when the Japanese launched nearly 400 sorties against the American fleet off the Marianas. US carrier-borne aircraft shot down 300 enemy planes, and submarines soon sank the carriers *Taiho* and *Shokaku*. It was a total disaster for the Japanese and was one of the most one-sided battles of the Second World War. Here, the Japanese carrier *Chiyoda* is hit aft during the US air attacks.

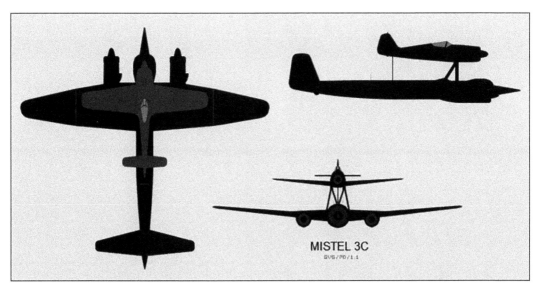

MISTEL 3C

On 24 June, the Germans introduced a new weapon against the fleet still lying off the Normandy coast. This was the Mistel, a pilotless aircraft or bomb carried piggyback and then launched from a JU88. Luckily for the Allies, the attackers mistook old hulks being used as breakwaters for ships. This plan or diagram shows how the device worked.

*Opposite*: The Americans launched an assault to take the strategically important port of Cherbourg on 22 June. It took five days to capture the town and port, which were badly damaged – much of the damage being caused by German forces before they surrendered. A navy diver is lowered into the water to check on damage to the harbour installations at Cherbourg.

# July

The battleship *Rodney*, which was called into action on 7 July to use its guns in a bombardment of German positions in and around Caen.

The cruiser *Black Prince* returns to port after taking part in the bombardment of Cherbourg.

Corsair fighter bombers on the deck of a carrier. These American-built aircraft were capable of speeds higher than 250 miles per hour – a far cry from the slow and unwieldy Swordfish, which were the backbone of the Fleet Air Arm for many years.

The submarine HMS *Tactician* returns to port after a cruise that saw her sink two merchant ships and become involved with five special operations.

US Avenger bombers on the flight deck of a British carrier.

A Russian liaison officer watches operations from the bridge of the escort carrier *Fencer*.

Reinforcements for the armies fighting in Normandy are shipped out in a landing craft. Flat-bottomed and liable to roll in any type of sea, it must have been an uncomfortable trip for the soldiers in the LCIs.

The frigate HMS *Holmes* with a Hunt-class destroyer, *Southdown*, astern.

# August

A Fairmile MTB at sea.

The destroyer *Raider*, the photograph taken from the accompanying battleship *Warspite*.

On 15 August, Allied forces landed in the south of France, between Marseilles and Nice, in a follow-up operation to the D-Day landings. Over 800 ships of varying size and type supported the invading force, which quickly established itself on French soil.

German prisoners after the Allied landings in the south of France. A landing craft waits in the background, presumably to transport the prisoners out of the battle zone.

Some of the crew of HMS *Ultimatum*, which sank over 6,000 tons of enemy shipping in the Mediterranean.

The forward gun of a Russian warship operating in the Black Sea. By August 1944, the Russians had won the sea war in the Black Sea – it was just a question of when the German Navy would pull out.

# September

The oil tanker *Tafelberg* had been mined in the Bristol Channel in 1941. In the process of being towed to safety, she broke in two and came ashore at Porthkerry near Barry. There the two halves of the ship remained for many months.

With the need for merchant vessels as great as ever, in 1943 the two halves of the *Tafelberg* were taken into Cardiff and welded together. Renamed as the *Empire Heritage*, she sailed again in 1943. Unfortunately, she was an unlucky vessel and the repaired ship was torpedoed and sunk off Malin Head on 8 September 1944. Over 100 passengers and crew went down with her.

Fleet Admiral Chester Nimitz, commander-in-chief of the American Pacific Fleet.

Churchill, Roosevelt and their chiefs of staff at the Second Quebec Conference, 12 September 1944. This was where the two leaders laid out their objectives for what they hoped was the final stage of the war against Germany and Japan.

The Royal Indian Navy sloop *Jumna*, one of several similar vessels operating around the Indian coast.

A Fleet Air Arm attack on a German convoy.

Part of the harbour and dock at Antwerp, a vital port for bringing in supplies to the Allied armies. An attack on the gates of the dock by German frogmen in September hampered Allied progress in the land war.

A crashed Barracuda on the flight deck of HMS *Rajah*.

An aerial view of an attack on an enemy ship in the Aegean Sea.

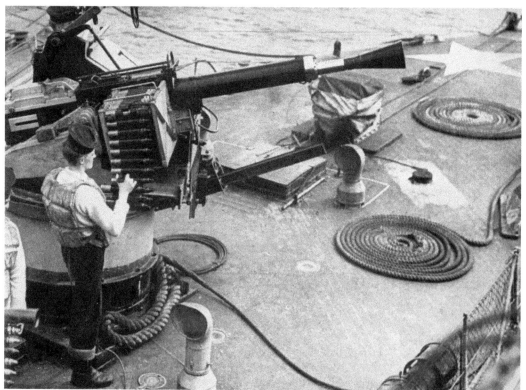

Sea on land! Heavy rains in the autumn of 1944 caused the River Maas to overflow, making life unbearable for military and civilians alike.

*Opposite above*: A Corsair makes an emergency landing on the deck of a British carrier during an attack on Sigli in Sumatra, 18 September 1944. Dramatically, the petrol tank detached from the plane and burst into flames; however, the fire was soon put out.

*Opposite below*: A gun crew on a British MTB.

# October

The Australian cruiser *Canberra* was badly damaged by Japanese bomb attacks on 12 October, during an attack on Formosa. Here we see her still firing, despite the damage suffered during these aerial assaults.

On 20 October, US forces landed at Leyte. General MacArthur, ever aware of the value of publicity, was photographed wading ashore.

The Battle of Leyte Gulf began on 22 October and lasted for three full days. During this time, the Japanese battleship *Musashi* – one of the largest and most powerful in the world – was sunk by US carrier aircraft. Two Japanese aircraft carriers sank with her. The USS *Princetown* was badly damaged in the battle, after being bombed by Japanese land-based aircraft; it is pictured here while on fire.

From the autumn of 1944, British naval forces became increasingly involved in the Pacific war. This shows Seafire aircraft on the deck of the carrier *Victorious*.

An artist's impression of an attack by Lancasters on the *Tirpitz*, 29 October 1944. As they feared a Russian attack, the German High Command had moved the ship from Altafjord to Tromso Fjord on 15 October. The move put *Tirpitz* 100 miles closer to British airfields and made RAF attacks even more likely.

US troops come ashore at Leyte.

The forward guns of the US battleship *Iowa*, as seen from the ship's bridge.

Sailors look at the memorial plaque to Captain John Walker (or Johnny Walker, as he was known, after the whiskey). Walker sank more U-boats than any other Allied commander during the Battle of the Atlantic, but died of a cerebral thrombosis in July 1944 – possibly brought on by strain and overwork.

*Opposite*: Captain and crew on the conning tower of a Royal Navy submarine.

The King, on one of his many inspection visits to RN establishments. This time he is visiting the training base HMS *Excellent*. The old wooden-wall *Victory* sits in the background.

The USS *Princetown*, seriously damaged at the Battle of Leyte Gulf.

Seafires and Wildcats on the deck of HMS *Formidable*, after she had joined the Pacific Fleet.

A mine explodes close to the river bank, as the Scheldt is being cleared to enable Antwerp to be used by Allied forces.

A Japanese aircraft – identifiable only by the plume of smoke – is shot down, and crashes into the sea during the Battle of the Sibuyan Sea, 24 October.

This shows the giant Japanese battleship *Yamoto* hit by bombs in the Battle of the Sibuyan Sea. Despite the damage, she survived – this time.

# November

The Japanese battleship *Kongo*, torpedoed and sunk by the USS *Sealion* on 21 November, just north of Formosa.

The aircraft carrier *Shinano*, sunk off Honshu. With limited destroyer escorts, the Japanese capital ships were increasingly vulnerable to torpedo attack.

A British minesweeper comes cautiously up the Scheldt, as Dutch civilians wave in welcome.

With the Scheldt clear of mines, Antwerp, yet another port on the continent of Europe, became available for use by the Allies.

HMS *Graph*, which was previously a U-boat. It was captured by the Royal Navy and recommissioned.

The destruction of the *Tirpitz* – at last. Her threat had always been more significant than the damage she did, but the sinking of the giant battleship, sister ship to the *Bismark*, was a relief to all naval planners.

A casualty being transferred from a motorboat to the cruiser *Orion*.

German motorboats found after the Allied forces landed at Flushing. They sit on trailers, left behind and abandoned when German troops hurriedly pulled out.

Russian patrol boats operating in the Baltic Sea.

Sailors on board a minesweeper take pot shots at a loose mine. It needed a steady arm and good eyes to detonate a floating mine in this way.

The war, in some people's eyes at least, might be nearly over, but ships were still needed. This shows the launch of a new warship for the Royal Navy.

# December

On 13 December, the cruiser *Nashville* was severely damaged by a kamikaze plane that smashed into her deck.

Christmas dinner on the mess deck.

A Seafire with wings folded, on the deck of her carrier.

A US aircraft carrier under attack in the Pacific.

HMS *Norfolk* refuels a US destroyer in the middle of the Pacific Ocean.

The battleship *Howe* became the flagship of Admiral Sir Bruce Fraser, the newly appointed commander-in-chief of the British Pacific Fleet for the final stages of the war against Japan.

Aircraft handlers carefully manoeuvre a Barracuda into position, prior to take off.

Anti-aircraft bursts in the sky above a US destroyer, during a landing on one of the Pacific islands.

Japanese shipping in the harbour at Manilla comes under attack from US carrier-borne bombers.

Gunners on HMS *Berwick*.

The aircraft carrier *Furious*, her flight deck swept by rough seas.

Gunners on a US warship arm rockets for use against Japanese land forces.

Aircraft might have come to assume a significant role in anti-submarine warfare, but there was still room – and a desperate need – for surface ships to carry on the campaign against the enemy submarines, whether they were German or Japanese. And depth charges remained a vital weapon.

Minesweepers returning to base, after a day clearing enemy mines from the North Sea.

British aircraft carriers in the Pacific.

# ALSO AVAILABLE FROM AMBERLEY PUBLISHING

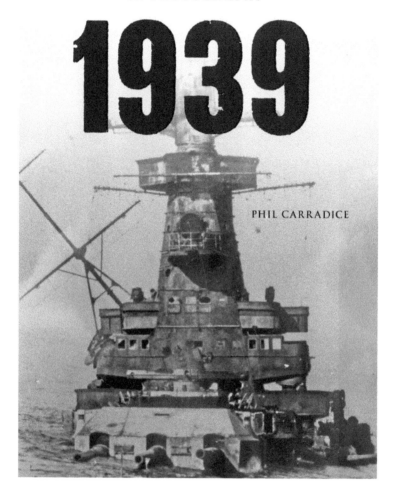

1939: The Second World War at Sea in Photographs

Phil Carradice

In the first of a series of books, naval expert Phil Carradice takes us through the war at sea in 1939 using previously unpublished and rare images of the battles, the ships and the people involved.

978 1 4456 2235 4
144 pages, illustrated throughout

Available from all good bookshops or order direct
from our website www.amberley-books.com

# ALSO AVAILABLE FROM AMBERLEY PUBLISHING

1940: The Second World War at Sea in Photographs

Phil Carradice

Using many rarely seen images, Phil Carradice tells the story of 1940 at sea.

978 1 4456 2240 8
144 pages, illustrated throughout

Available from all good bookshops or order direct
from our website www.amberley-books.com

# ALSO AVAILABLE FROM AMBERLEY PUBLISHING

### THE SECOND WORLD WAR AT SEA IN PHOTOGRAPHS

# 1941

#### PHIL CARRADICE

1941: The Second World War at Sea in Photographs

Phil Carradice

In 1941, Britain stood alone. North Africa dominated the news. Bismarck sank Hood. Fortress Britain endured the Blitz. Russia was invaded. Japan woke the USA with its attack on Pearl Harbor.

978 1 4456 2245 3
136 pages, illustrated throughout

Available from all good bookshops or order direct
from our website www.amberley-books.com

# ALSO AVAILABLE FROM AMBERLEY PUBLISHING

### THE SECOND WORLD WAR AT SEA IN PHOTOGRAPHS

# 1942

#### PHIL CARRADICE

1942: The Second World War at Sea in Photographs

Phil Carradice

A unique look at the fourth year of the Second World War at sea, through the medium of old photographs.

978 1 4456 2249 1
144 pages, illustrated throughout

Available from all good bookshops or order direct from our website www.amberley-books.com

ALSO AVAILABLE FROM AMBERLEY PUBLISHING

THE SECOND WORLD WAR AT SEA
IN PHOTOGRAPHS

# 1943

PHIL CARRADICE

1943: The Second World War at Sea in Photographs

Phil Carradice

Phil Carradice looks at the fourth year of the Second World War at sea, through the medium of old and rare photographs.

978 1 4456 2252 1
144 pages, illustrated throughout

Available from all good bookshops or order direct
from our website www.amberley-books.com